**W9-BFM-150**

# COLONIAL LIFE IN AMERICA

A BOOK TO BEGIN ON

# COLONIAL LIFE

Holt, Rinehart and Winston

New York / Chicago / San Francisco

# IN AMERICA

Margaret C. Farquhar

Illustrated by Ed Emberley

Published simultaneously in Canada by Holt, Rinehart
and Winston of Canada, Limited.

Library of Congress Catalog Card Number: 62–14816

*Designer: Nonny Hogrogian*
92747–0312
Printed in the United States of America

Columbus discovered America in 1492.

Later, other explorers visited the new land. They told people in Europe of the forests, furs, and fish they found.

Many Europeans decided to settle in this wonderful land.

But some of the first settlers starved to death during the hard winters.

Others lived to build settlements or colonies for their mother countries.

Colonial America was beginning.

In 1607, three ships brought men from England to what is now Jamestown, Virginia. They were looking for gold.

The leader, Captain John Smith, taught the men to build houses of stakes and branches. They plastered the walls of the houses with mud. The roofs were thatched with straw and rushes.

The colonists found no gold in Virginia. But they did find forests.

The men learned to split logs into long boards, called clapboards.

They sent the clapboards in ships to England. They were used there for building houses.

In exchange, the colonists were sent food and clothing.

The colonists discovered that tobacco plants grew wild in Virginia. Indians smoked the dried leaves, which were bitter and strong.

Soon the colonists learned to grow a better kind of tobacco.

People in England bought this new, sweet tobacco for their pipes.

More settlers came from Europe to Virginia, Maryland, and the Carolinas to plant tobacco.

After many years, there were tobacco plantations along the rivers and in the back country of these Southern colonies.

Every large plantation had a wharf on a river. At the wharf, barrels of tobacco were loaded on ships and carried down to the ocean, on their way to England.

The tobacco was sold in the mother country. Then the ships—filled with crates of fine clothing, furniture, and silverware—returned to the plantations.

These colonists no longer lived in mud and straw huts.

They built large clapboard or brick houses on their plantations.

The Southern plantation owners had slaves to work in the tobacco fields and in the houses.

Slaves also worked in the rice fields of South Carolina, and later, in the cotton fields of Georgia.

Traders brought the slaves from Africa and sold them to the colonists.

A large plantation in the South was like a village.

Slave families had their own cabins.

There were shops for brickmakers and carpenters. There was a dairy for making butter and a smokehouse for curing hams.

Some plantations had a schoolhouse. The owner hired a tutor to teach his children.

Families from the plantations visited each other for several days at a time. Because plantations were so far apart, the trip took a long time.

The women came in coaches pulled by horses. The men rode horseback.

In the evenings, everyone danced the Virginia reel in the ballroom of the plantation house.

In 1620, thirteen years after the Jamestown Colony was settled, the Pilgrims sailed to America in their ship, the *Mayflower.*

They came to build a church where they could worship God in their own way.

The Pilgrims named their landing place Plymouth, after their home in England. This new Plymouth was in another part of America called New England.

The first houses in Plymouth were
built on a narrow street leading up a hill.
Each house had only one room with a
large stone fireplace.

At the top of the hill, looking over the
sea, the Pilgrims built their church. They
called it a meeting house.

The Pilgrims chopped down oak and pine trees to make benches and beds.

One kind of bench was called a settle. The settle had a high back to keep off drafts.

The children sat on stools or stood at the table to eat.

A musket hung over every fireplace.

Children slept in a trundle bed. This was a small cot, which was stored under the large bed during the day.

A baby would sleep in a cradle near the fireplace.

There were no closets in the houses. The Pilgrims kept their clothes in deep chests.

The Pilgrims had few utensils for
cooking and eating. In some houses, a
whole family used one wooden trencher.
A trencher is a scooped-out wooden plate.

They had a few wooden and pewter
spoons, but no forks. Meat was eaten
with their fingers.

They drank cider from wooden mugs.

The Indians taught the Pilgrims to fish and to plant corn.

They showed the Pilgrims how to grind corn into meal, and to make hasty pudding and corn cake.

They taught the Pilgrims to tap maple trees and boil the sap into maple sugar.

On week days, the Pilgrim men wore bright-colored stocking caps and knitted stockings. They wore linen shirts and knee breeches.

The women wore tight bodices and full skirts that came to their ankles. They had long aprons and little white caps.

On Sundays, both men and women wore tall beaver hats with wide brims. A few Pilgrims had bright red capes.

A drummer beat a signal and the Pilgrims marched to church together. There, they listened to long sermons.

No one worked or played on Sunday.

The Pilgrims brought a few chickens and pigs on the *Mayflower*. There was no room to bring cows.

They ate wild turkey, deer meat, and fish. For two years, they had no beef to eat or cow's milk to drink.

At last, a ship brought two cows and a bull. Sheep and horses were sent to America on later ships.

After a few years, the Pilgrims built larger houses with two floors. Each room had its own fireplace.

Every house had a barn for cattle and a shed for hay.

The Pilgrims were satisfied with their new home in America.

In 1630, ten years after the Pilgrims had landed at Plymouth, the Puritans sailed from England to America.

They settled first in what is now Boston, not very far from Plymouth.

These Puritans did not stay together for long. Many of them moved to other parts of New England to build new towns.

The Puritans built their houses and shops around a meeting house, or church.

No one could live in a Puritan town if he did not belong to the church.

The Puritan fathers met there to make the town laws. Men who broke the laws were punished by being made to sit in the stocks.

Every morning at sunrise, the Puritans drove their cows to the town pasture called a common. Every night at sundown, they drove the cattle home again.

Oxen did the heavy work on the farms. They hauled loads of stone and wood in two-wheeled carts. They pulled wooden ploughs through the fields.

The blacksmith made iron shoes on his forge for the oxen and horses. He also made iron nails and tools.

The Pilgrims and Puritans had a Thanksgiving Day, and at harvest time, they had corn-husking bees.

They had fairs on the village green.

The men bowled and ran races. Children played blind-man's buff and stool-ball with a leather ball full of feathers.

Some of the Puritans who lived on the Atlantic sea coast built trading ships and fishing boats.

They used white pine for the ships' tall masts.

The trading ships carried lumber and fur overseas. They brought back sugar, molasses, spices, and household goods.

Fishermen caught codfish off the coast of New England. They dried and salted the cod, and shipped it to Europe.

Whalers went to sea in whaling vessels.

Whale oil was used to burn in lamps.

In 1623, a ship brought the first Dutch people to live in America. They came to trade with the Indians for furs.

The Dutch settled along the Hudson River and on Long Island. They also settled Manhattan Island.

Like the other early settlers, the Dutch first lived in wooden huts.

They, too, ate corn, game, and fish.

The Dutch settlers shipped back furs to their homeland, the Netherlands. Soon, they were sent horses, cattle, and sheep. Cocoa, spices, food, and clothing were also sent.

After a few years, they built narrow, brick houses, like the ones they had left in the Netherlands.

Around many of the houses were gardens with tulips and hyacinths growing in them.

Some of the Dutch had shops in their houses. They sold beaver hats with plumes, wooden shoes, and toys.

Tiny shells called wampum were used for money.

After the day's work was finished, the people sat on their stoops or porches until the curfew rang at eight o'clock.

Then watchmen with rattles walked through the streets. The sound of the rattles meant all was well.

Some of the Dutch people lived on neat farms along the Hudson River.

They built windmills to grind their corn and grain.

In winter, they had sleighing and skating parties.

The Dutch gave presents to their children on the Eve of Saint Nicholas.

Other people settled on the land between Virginia and New York.

The Swedish ruler sent people to begin a colony for Sweden in Delaware.

An English Quaker, William Penn, wanted to worship God in his own way. He and other Quakers began to settle Philadelphia in 1683.

The Quakers built square houses of stone, brick, or wood, in Philadelphia.

One of the first things they built was a school. Quaker and Indian children studied reading, writing, and arithmetic together. Boys were taught to make shoes and furniture. Girls learned to spin and do needlework.

People began to come to America from Germany, too.

Some of the German settlers moved into the back country of Pennsylvania. There, they raised cattle and wheat.

They built stone houses and barns. They painted flowers on their furniture and dishes. Special marks called hex signs were put on the doors of their barns to bring good luck.

Pennsylvania Germans were among the best farmers of all the colonists.

# THE THIRTEEN COLONIES

Pennsylvania

MD

Virginia

North Carolina

South Carolina

Georgia

New York

New Hampshire

Maine
{ then part of MASS. }

Mass.

Conn.

R.I.

N.J

Del.

England owned a large amount of the land in America. But the King wanted even more.

His soldiers captured New York, New Jersey, and Delaware.

By 1733, England owned thirteen colonies in America.

The King of England sent a governor to each of these colonies. The people had to obey the English governor's orders.

In many ways, life was the same in all thirteen colonies.

All colonial women cooked over fireplaces.

An oven was built into the side of the chimney. Once a week, it was heated with coals. Beans, bread, and corn cakes were baked in the oven.

Strings of dried apple, cherries, and pumpkin hung from the mantle, ready for stewing.

The colonists saved melted fat and wood ashes to make lye soap.

They dipped strings of twisted hemp or cotton into melted fat to make candles for light.

Many women kept herb gardens. They grew sage and onions to flavor their meats. Rosemary and sweet-smelling herbs were put in linen chests. Some herbs were ground into medicines.

The colonial people grew flax to make thread for linen cloth. They raised sheep for their wool.

Every spring, the men and boys sheared the sheep. Then they washed the fleece.

Grandmothers and children carded the wool. They pulled the bent wire teeth of the cards through the fleece, until it was soft and fluffy.

The spinning wheel twisted strands of wool into yarn.

The women dipped the yarn into a kettle of boiling dye.

The indigo plant made very strong dye. It colored the wool blue. Birch bark and pokeweed berries made yellow and red dyes.

Now the yarn was ready to be knitted into stockings and mittens or woven into cloth on a large loom.

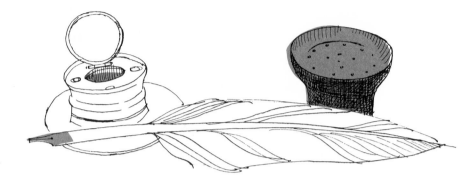

Postriders began to carry mail on horseback over Indian trails from one colony to another.

Men wrote letters with a goose quill pen on paper made from linen rags. They blotted the ink by sprinkling it with sand from a shaker.

There were no envelopes. The letters were folded and sealed with a drop of melted wax.

Later, the postriders carried news sheets printed in Boston, Philadelphia, and Virginia.

Men in Boston read in the news sheets that Virginians wanted to be free to rule themselves.

The Virginians read that the New Englanders felt the same way.

On July 4, 1776, men from the thirteen English colonies met in Philadelphia. There they signed the Declaration of Independence.

Then, the colonists fought the long Revolutionary War with England and won their independence.

At last the colonists were free to rule themselves.

Now they could call their country the United States of America.

MARGARET C. FARQUHAR's interest in colonial life is a personal one, for a Puritan ancestor of hers settled in Massachusetts in 1630. She holds a B.A. degree from the University of Michigan, an M.A. from Columbia University, and an M.S. in Library Science from Western Reserve. Her work as a library consultant for elementary and junior high schools in Fairfield, Connecticut, has led her to write both *Colonial Life in America* and *Lights,* her first Book to Begin On.

ED EMBERLEY visited the restored colonial villages, Sturbridge Village, Plimouth Plantation, and Salem, and sketched the houses and objects there for this book. A graduate of the Massachusetts School of Art, he lives north of Boston with his wife and two young children. His first book for children, *The Wing on a Flea,* was chosen by the New York *Times* as one of the ten best illustrated children's books of 1961.